THIS COLOURING MAGAZINE BELONGS TO

____

COVER AND INTERIOR ILLUSTRATIONS BY
SIRREESE AND A. CLARKE
TEXT BY A. CLARKE.

MEET THE RENAISSANCE FEMALES

WWW.SIRREESE.COM

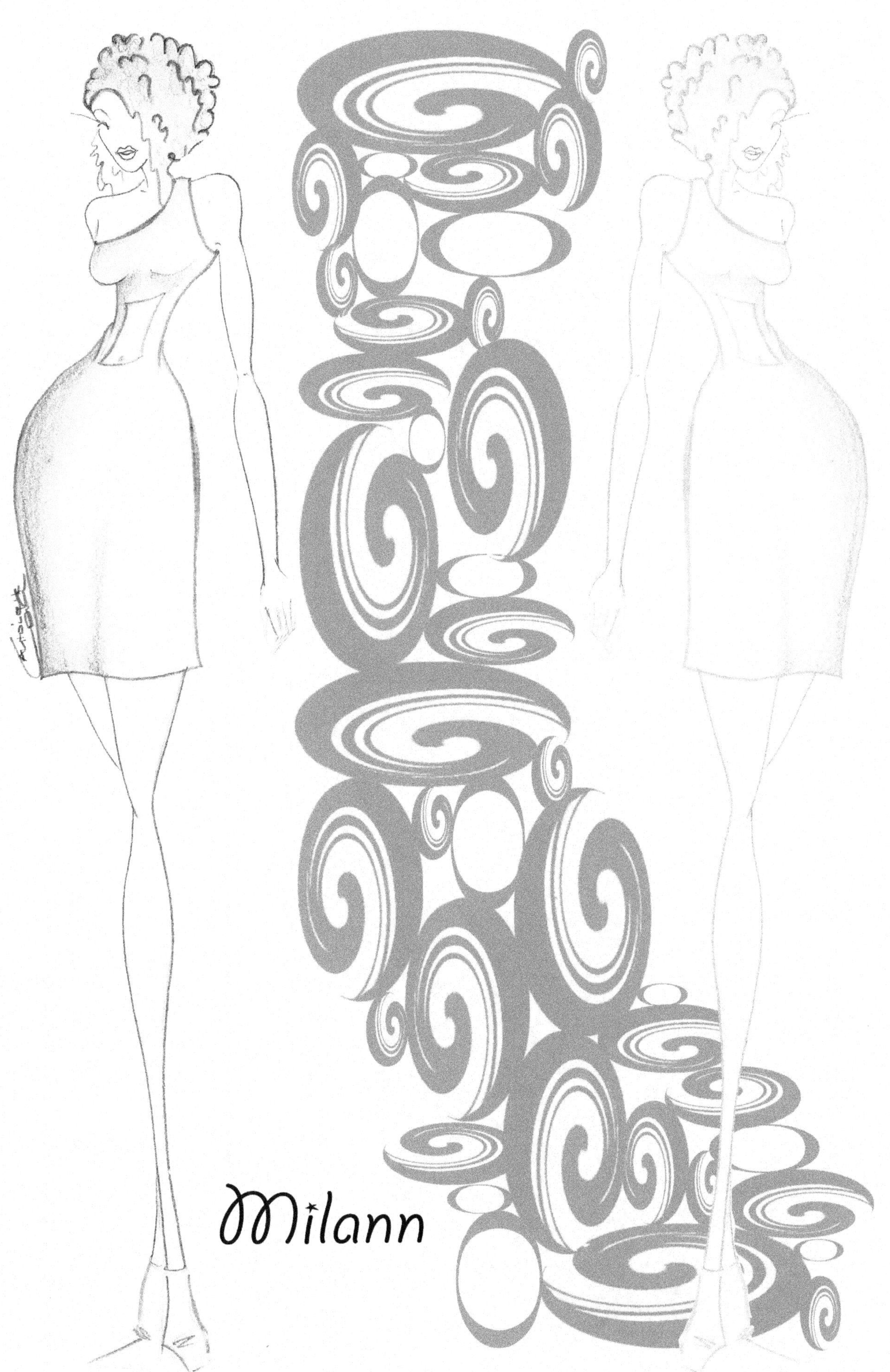

Milann

Angelees

LONDONN

PARISS

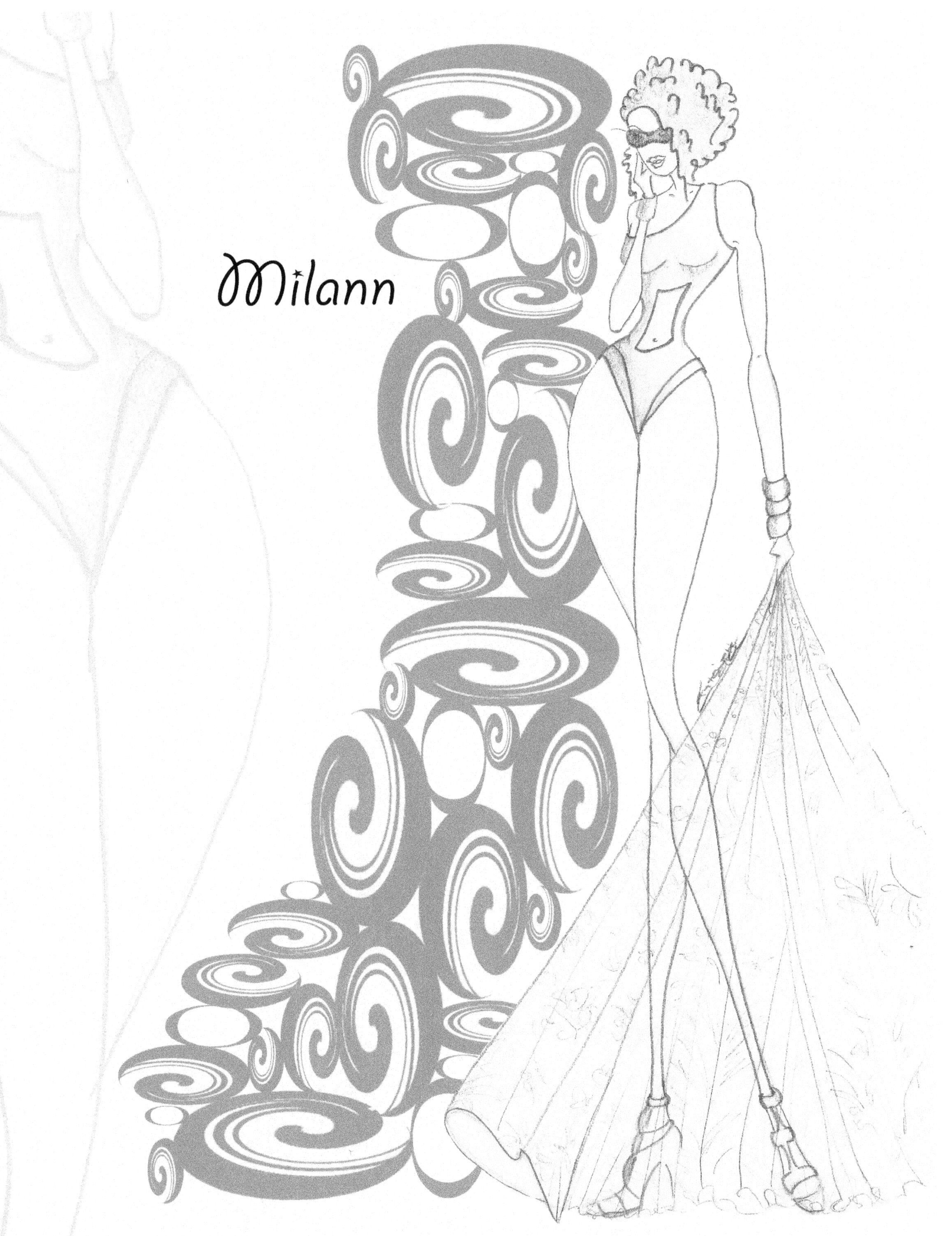

Milann

PARISS

Dunn's River Falls

Dunn's River Falls is one of the most popular tourist attractions in Jamaica and the Caribbean. At about 155m high and 180m long, the waterfalls are terraced like giant natural staircase. The staggering falls are surrounded by thick, lush, green vegetation that provides shade and keeps the area and visitors cool. Climbing is a popular pastime at Dunn's River Falls.

There are stairs alongside of the falls, for those who do not want to get wet or are unable to manage the rocky and uneven terrain of the actual waterfall

Devon House

Devon House Mansion is one of Jamaica's most celebrated historical landmarks, sitting on 11 lush acres in the capital city it represents the island's cultural diversity and was constructed in the 19th century for George Stiebel, Jamaica's first black millionaire. Stiebel was among three wealthy Jamaicans who constructed elaborate homes during the late 19th century, which fittingly became known as the Millionaires Corner. Daniel Finzi and the Verleys were the other families that resided in the area, however, both homes were eventually demolished to make way for development.

With original Furnishings and a collection of 19th-century antiques from Jamaica and the Caribbean region, the ballroom still has the original English chandelier purchased by Stiebel for the room. Stiebel's legacy lives on with the beautifully maintained Devon House, which was declared a national monument in 1990 by the Jamaica National Heritage Trust.

Bob Marley Museum

The Bob Marley Museum is the former residence and music studio of the legendary reggae singer, Bob Marley. Located in Jamaica's capital Kingston, it was home to Mr. Marley until his death in 1981.

You may run into one of his sons who often visit to use the studio!

A tour shows a very personal view of Bob's life, history and philosophy of his music, it also tells the story of Bob Marley's life after he moved uptown." Although the home is very simplistic, vibrant Rastafarian murals and colours decorate the surroundings, in the home are Rastafarian religious cloaks and Bob Marley's favourite denim shirt.

Bob Marley Museum

A statue of the music legend is at the entrance. When browsing inside, you will see many of Marley's prestigious awards and a displays of Bob's gold and platinum records along the walls and the Order of Merit given to him by the Jamaican government.
One of the rooms showcases media clippings of Marley's superstar life.

The most intriguing room of all is Marley's unadorned bedroom left just as it was with his star-shaped guitar laying beside his bed. It was in this bedroom that a failed assassination attempt was made on Bob Marley

Bob Marley Museum

Although Bob Marley passed away at a very young age, his memory lives on forever not only in Jamaica but all over the world.

National Heroes Park

National Heroes Park located on what was once a popular horse-racing centre and an area for celebrating various events. The National Heroes Park was officially so designated in 1973. The prominent feature of the park is The Jamaica War Memorial, a cenotaph honouring the Jamaicans killed in combat during World War I and World War II.

This botanical garden spot is also the burial place of many of the nation's Prime Ministers. It is now a permanent place for honouring national heroes with monuments established in an area known as The Shrine.

Marcus Mosiah Garvey, Nanny of the Maroons, Samuel Sharpe, Sir William Alexander Bustamante, and Norman Washington Manley are all honoured here. The park is used for concerts and other events throughout the year.

Garvey's name is synonymous internationally with black nationalism and racial pride, he created a revolution of black nationalism and consciousness. Born on August 17, 1887, Jamaica's first National Hero overcame opposition in his own land to inspire millions worldwide.

His teachings were instrumental in the fight for independence in several African States as well as in social reform in the United States during the 1940s and 50s. Mr Garvey's motto was

"One God, One Aim, One Destiny"

Nanny of the Maroons

Nanny of the Maroons, a female warrior of Asante descent who waged a guerrilla campaign against the British. These guerrilla warriors – slaves who escaped from the plantations and made their homes in the woodlands of Jamaica's interior, hold pride of place in constant, unyielding attacks on the British colonialists. Under the guidance of Nanny, the group actively raided and plundered and gave slaves their freedom. Both her followers and the British feared Nanny. There are also documented accounts of her prowess as a military strategist in the First Maroon War, 1720 to 1739. Jamaicans recognize her unique contribution to the struggle for full freedom of the enslaved population, finally achieved in 1838. Nanny has been given Jamaica's highest honour, National Hero (Heroine). A portrait of Nanny can be found on the Jamaican five-hundred-dollar bill. Nanny's monument reproduces the sound of the Abeng, a traditional instrument used by the fighters.

Milann

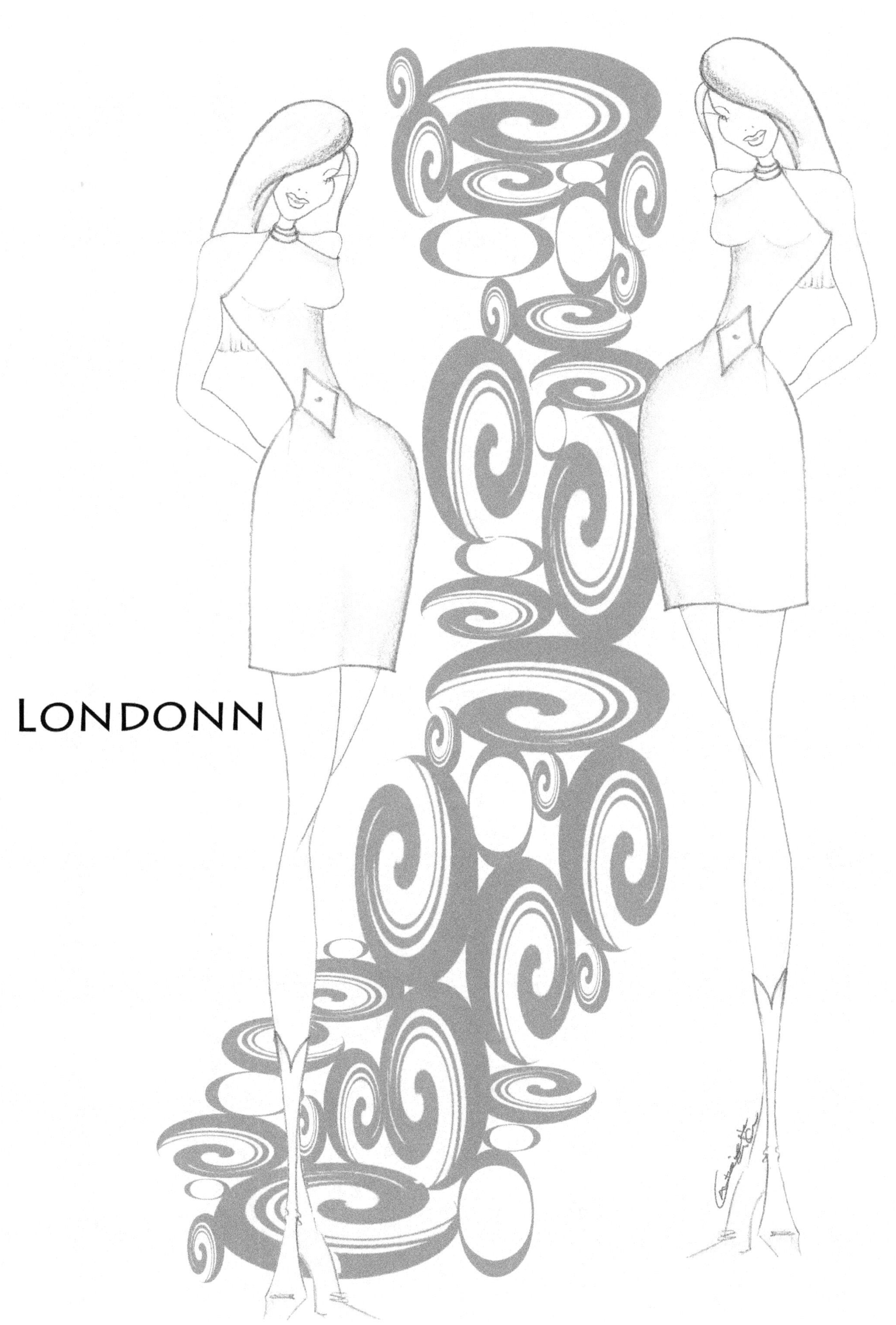

LONDONN

Angelees

LONDONN

PARISS

Angelees

www.ingramcontent.com/pod-product-compliance
Lightning Source LLC
Chambersburg PA
CBHW080047260726
48658CB00007B/2789